foreseen.
forgiven.
FREE.

Freedom Is Waiting ...

Michele Coomer

WESTBOW
PRESS®
A DIVISION OF THOMAS NELSON
& ZONDERVAN

Scripture taken from the Holy Bible, NEW INTERNATIONAL VERSION®. Copyright © 1973, 1978, 1984 by Biblica, Inc. All rights reserved worldwide. Used by permission. NEW INTERNATIONAL VERSION® and NIV® are registered trademarks of Biblica, Inc. Use of either trademark for the offering of goods or services requires the prior written consent of Biblica US, Inc.

Scripture taken from the New King James Version. Copyright © 1979, 1980, 1982 by Thomas Nelson, Inc. Used by permission. All rights reserved.

WestBow Press books may be ordered through booksellers or by contacting:

WestBow Press
A Division of Thomas Nelson & Zondervan
1663 Liberty Drive
Bloomington, IN 47403
www.westbowpress.com
1 (866) 928-1240

Because of the dynamic nature of the Internet, any web addresses or links contained in this book may have changed since publication and may no longer be valid. The views expressed in this work are solely those of the author and do not necessarily reflect the views of the publisher, and the publisher hereby disclaims any responsibility for them.

Any people depicted in stock imagery provided by Thinkstock are models, and such images are being used for illustrative purposes only. Certain stock imagery © Thinkstock.

ISBN: 978-1-4908-8668-8 (sc)
ISBN: 978-1-4908-8667-1 (e)

Library of Congress Control Number: 2015910521

Print information available on the last page.

WestBow Press rev. date: 08/07/2015

Contents

for Mark, who introduced me to Jesus,
the One who set me free

Introduction

Whether we admit it or not, most of us have or have had something in our lives that put us in chains and kept us from walking in freedom. As a child I was held in physical and emotional bondage. As an adult, I no longer experienced that form of bondage, but I was still not walking in freedom. I was bound by chains of fear, shame, and perfectionism. I did everything I could to make my life look perfect so that no one would suspect the story I was hiding.

Maybe you don't call it bondage, and so you don't recognize it. Try framing it like this: What do you have in your life that is keeping you from living it to the fullest? What demands of your time? Your energy? Your finances?

This book is unique in that it serves as an interactive study. As I share the Biblical truths that God revealed to me on my journey and relate my own personal story, I will also guide you on your own journey to freedom. In this study we will take a look at some of the many places in scripture where God shows us that He is the One who breaks our chains and grants us freedom to live the life He intended for us to live. We will learn that the events in our lives were foreseen by the Creator of the universe. We will learn that in all things we are forgiven and that Christ is the only way to that forgiveness. Finally, we will learn what it means to walk in freedom.

God has granted me freedom, and every day I have the privilege of walking in it. I am so glad that you have chosen to go on this journey with me. Freedom is waiting.

About this Book

I hope that you are ready for life change. This book is going to take you into deeper knowledge of the Word, deeper relationship with the Lord, and deeper understanding of yourself. I want you to let the Spirit guide the time you spend on each section of this book. I really want you to bask in His Holy Word. That might mean all you do one day is read the verses in a section and spend the rest of your time talking with God about what you've read. I have found that the most meaningful experiences I have had with the Lord turn out to be the ones where I throw out all time boundaries and let the Holy Spirit lead me.

This study is scripture intensive. You will sometimes read entire chapters in the Bible because I want you to read each passage in context. I want you to spend time meditating on the scripture passages. Look at each word. Does one stand out? What does it say? Spend time meditating on your answers to the questions. If you want to experience life change, then dig deep. Dare to look at the things in your life you might otherwise overlook. Ask God to show you the places in your life where you need to find freedom. Ask God to reveal Himself to you through His Word. To get the most out of this study you will want to spend time in prayerful consideration as to what the Lord wants you to learn from each passage. There will be questions in each section to help you respond to the scripture and guide you on your personal journey to freedom. Again, if you want to experience life change, dig deep. All of the passages referenced in this study are taken from The Holy Bible, New International Version.

Hebrews 4:12 says, "For the word of God is living and active. Sharper than any double edged sword, it penetrates even to dividing soul and spirit, joints and marrow; it judges the thoughts and attitudes of the heart." His Word is living. It is life-changing. We can't simply just read the Word. We must let it change our lives.

part one. foreseen.

foreseen. known beforehand; predetermined; seen in advance.

"For those God foreknew He also predestined to be conformed to the likeness of His Son, that He might be the firstborn among many brothers. And those He predestined, He also called; those He called, He also justified; those he justified, He also glorified."

Romans 8:29-30

God's ultimate goal is for us to be like Christ. As we become more like Christ, we discover our true selves, the persons we were created to be.

What appeared to be so normal to the world was so abnormal behind closed doors. He worked all day, drank until late into the night, then passed out until morning only to start the insanity all over again. She slept all day and was gone many nights. As a result I was left to raise myself, fending for my own meals before I was five years old. When they were both at home there was constant fighting, almost always ending violently. When he was in a drunken rage no one was safe, myself included. My earliest childhood memory is of being thrown from a Sit-and-Spin by him when I was three years old. She sent me off to my room to stay out of the way.

The sexual abuse began when I was a young child. She would lock him out of her bedroom and he would abuse me in the room right next door. I desperately wanted her love and comfort, but she did not give it to me. I learned at a very young age that I was on my own. When I was nine he moved into an apartment. I was sent to the apartment every weekend, and every weekend I endured his abuse. At the apartment things went to a whole new level. He installed a lock on the outside of the bedroom door at the apartment and locked me inside the bedroom each weekend. Other men were invited to the room. I never knew the men that came or how many would come in a night. He drove me home on Sundays as if nothing happened.

Sometimes we would take road trips where he would sell me to other men. In Colorado I was sold to a man in a remote cabin. In Washington DC I was sold to a group of executives in a penthouse suite.

chapter 1. freedom is for everyone.

I love to ride my bike. I loved it as a child, and I still love to ride. I remember getting my first bike for Christmas when I was six years old. It was green with a flowered banana seat. I rode that bike everywhere until I was a teenager. I spent hours exploring my neighborhood and all of the surrounding neighborhoods. I rode to the park, the library, the local market, and the creek behind the elementary school. I could be gone for hours on end and no one worried.

Things inside the walls of my very normal-looking house were anything but normal. When I was inside, I felt trapped and afraid, never knowing when the next violent outburst would occur or what else might happen. Whenever I could escape the house, I would get on my bike and pedal all of my fears away. My bike gave me a sense of freedom.

Think back to your childhood. How would you describe it?

_____

_____

_____

_____

_____

What made you feel carefree and gave you a sense of freedom?

_____

_____

_____

Freedom is for everyone. God wants us to live in freedom, but He doesn't guarantee that it will come without difficulty or in our timeframe. Sometimes our journey to freedom may be long and arduous, leaving us wondering if freedom even exists.

God knows our pain.

Read Exodus 1 and 2. If you know this story, try to read it with fresh eyes. If you write in your Bible (and I hope you do), underline the words and phrases that stand out to you. Even if you don't know why they stand out, mark them anyway. After you read through the passage once, go back and review the things you marked. Meditate on them, and ask the Lord what you are supposed to learn from those words and phrases. Sometimes what God wants us to learn is summed up in one little word, but we must be sensitive to the Holy Spirit to hear Him point out that word.

Use the space below to journal what you learned or what the Lord said to you in your reading.

_____

_____

_____

_____

_____

Look back at Exodus 1:14. What was the result of the Egyptians' harsh treatment of the Israelites?

_____

_____

The Egyptian taskmasters treated the Israelites ruthlessly, and the Israelites became victims of their abuse and bitter because of it.

At the same time, the Hebrew women were experiencing their own bondage. They were in the midst of a horrible genocide. The Egyptian pharaoh had ordered all Hebrew male infants to be thrown into the Nile River. Imagine how trapped those women felt during their pregnancies, not knowing the fate of their unborn children. They would do anything to save their infant sons.

Besides being victimized and bitter, our bondage often makes us desperate. In fact, this is where we meet Moses in Exodus 2:1–3. His mother, in her desperation, made a waterproof basket for Moses and sent him down the river. As the story unfolds, we see this beautiful picture of what God had foreseen: a baby saved from genocide to save his people.

Maybe you experienced a difficult time in your life, and at that time, you couldn't see past the circumstance to envision a greater purpose. Yet God used that situation to bring about His glory. Or maybe you are going through a difficult time right now. Maybe your faith tells you that this time in your life has a bigger purpose, or maybe you are so entrenched in it that you can't see why God would possibly take you through this season. Write about it here.

_____

_____

_____

_____

_____

_____

Read Exodus 2:23–25. What do you learn from this passage about the character of God?

_____

_____

_____

The Israelites were not forgotten. Their cries went up to God. He heard them and remembered His covenant with their forefathers, Abraham, Isaac, and Jacob. Exodus 2:25 says that God was concerned about them.

What do you need to cry out to God today? What has you in bondage?

_____

_____

_____

_____

God hears your cries too, and He is concerned about you. He wants to bring you into the Promised Land. He wants you to be free.

God calls us to himself.

Read Exodus 3. Pay close attention to God's instructions and Moses' reply.

Pick one verse that really spoke to you from this passage. Use the space below to write that verse and journal about how it spoke to you.

_____

_____

_____

_____

_____

_____

What was Moses doing when he saw the flames inside the bush?

_____

_____

Moses was in the desert tending his flock, doing his day-to-day thing, when he saw the flames burning from within the bush. There are three things I want you to see about Moses' encounter with the bush.

First, Moses saw the bush. He wasn't so preoccupied with things in his life that he didn't notice it. Not only did he notice the bush but he also noticed that something was different about the bush, so he went to it. He didn't ignore it and pass it by. He didn't leave it for someone else to figure out. He went to it. You know, when God calls us to Himself, we have a choice to either move toward Him or away from Him. What do you do when God calls you?

Second, when the Lord spoke to him, Moses listened. He didn't pretend not to hear or understand. He didn't walk away midway through the conversation when things started to get tough. We have a choice when God speaks to us. Do you listen intently, or do you cover your ears?

Third, Moses was obedient. He wasn't all that excited about being chosen for the task ahead, and there wasn't room for interpretation on what to do because the Lord was very clear with His instructions, but Moses accepted the Lord's instruction. The Lord gives us clear instructions as well. Whether we want to follow them or not is irrelevant. Our choice is to be obedient or not.

Which of these three actions—moving, listening, or obeying—do you find the most difficult? Why?

_____

_____

_____

What things might cause you to miss the Lord's voice?

_____

_____

_____

When the Lord spoke to Moses, He not only gave him instructions but He also gave him the outcome. Moses may have been reluctant, but he did want the end result—freedom for his people.

So let's start with the end in mind as it pertains to this study. What does freedom look like to you? What kind of person would you be? If there were no obstacles, what would you do with your time? Your money? Where would you devote your energy? What would your relationships look like?

_____

_____

_____

_____

_____

God sends us on a life-journey.

Read Exodus 12.

Journal about the conditions under which Pharaoh let the Israelites go. What do you learn about God's divine plan from this passage?

_____

_____

_____

_____

_____

_____

The Lord is clear about what He wants us to do and the plan He has for our lives. The instructions for the Israelites regarding the Passover left no room for question or interpretation because they were very clear. He expects us to follow the plan He has laid out for our lives just as He expected the Israelites to follow His plan. In our obedience, God is faithful to keep His promises. He delivered the Israelites out of Egypt. He will deliver us, too.

Perhaps you've been on a life-journey, learning something about yourself, finding healing from an old wound, battling a chronic illness, or something else. How did it start?

_____

_____

_____

_____

_____

What obstacles did you face along the way or are you facing now?

_____

_____

_____

What have you learned from your journey so far?

_____

_____

_____

The Israelites were just beginning their journey, but they already had a foundation of the Lord's faithfulness. They had seen the signs and wonders the Lord had performed on their behalf. They saw the Nile River turned to blood and legions of frogs invade the land of Egypt. He demonstrated His power before their very eyes.

Where is God in your life-journey? Maybe you haven't thought about it. Use this time now to think about what you know of God and what you have seen Him do with your own eyes.

_____

_____

_____

God shows up. big.

Read Exodus 13:17–14:31

God was working big on the Israelites' behalf, and He wanted to make sure that they knew it was Him. So in a fashion that only God can pull off, He did things only He can do.

Look back at Exodus 13:21–22. How did God show up big to the Israelites in these verses?

_____

_____

When God is working in our lives, He doesn't want us to miss Him. What great comfort it must have been for the Israelites to have confirmation of the Lord's deliverance manifested in a visible pillar of cloud by day and a pillar of fire by night.

In what ways has God shown up big in your life?

_____

_____

_____

In the wake of their newfound freedom, and with a visible manifestation of the Lord's presence, the Israelites looked up and saw the Egyptian army charging after them. Exodus 14:10 says, "They were terrified and cried out to the Lord." And then they turned on Moses and blamed him for their plight, fearing that they would die in the desert at the hands of the Egyptian army. They even told Moses it would have been better for them to stay in Egypt.

We can grow content to live in our bondage because it is comfortable and familiar. We would rather stay comfortable than face the fear of freedom or the cost of obtaining it.

What does stepping into freedom look like for you? Telling your spouse about a past hurt? Confessing a hidden sin? Admitting that you can't do it all?

_____

_____

_____

_____

_____

I love that Moses does not lose faith in spite of his opposition. He says in Exodus 14:13, "Do not be afraid. Stand firm and you will see the deliverance the Lord will bring you today."

My favorite part of that verse is not where Moses says, "Do not be afraid," but where he says, "Stand firm." The command to not be afraid implies a passive response. The command to stand firm implies **action**. I learned something from these verses. God wants WAY more for us than to not be afraid. He wants us to have faith in His promises. He wants us to trust Him and what He says in His Word. He wants us to **stand firm**.

God uses this instruction many times in both the Old and New Testaments. In Exodus He tells us to '**stand firm** and see the deliverance of the Lord'. In 2 Chronicles He says that 'we will not have to fight the battle but to take our positions and **stand firm**'. He tells Job that he 'will **stand firm** and without fear'. The Psalmist writes that we are to 'rise up and **stand firm**'. In Proverbs, 'the righteous **stand firm** forever'. In Isaiah, 'if you don't **stand firm** you will not stand at all'. In Luke, 'by **standing firm** and you will gain life'. In 1 Corinthians, 'it is by faith that you **stand firm**'. In Ephesians He tells us to put on our Holy armor and '**stand firm** with the belt of Truth buckled on'. In Philippians, '**stand firm** and hold fast'. And in James, 'be patient and **stand firm**'.

So what does it mean to stand firm? Why are these two words so important? Think about it. When you stand firm, your feet are planted, and you are sure of the ground beneath you. You are standing up straight, confident in your stance. You are alert, ready for whatever may come; you won't be easily moved. God doesn't just want us to live passively unafraid. He wants us to actively, assertively, even aggressively **stand firm**.

What gives you the confidence to stand firm?

_____

_____

_____

Look again at Exodus 14:13. I don't want you to miss this truth. What does it say about the Egyptians?

_____

_____

What is the significance of this truth?

_____

_____

_____

"The Egyptians you see today you will *never* see again." The Egyptians were the Israelites' taskmasters. They represented their bondage, their chains. In this one verse, God guarantees deliverance. *Complete* deliverance. He said you will *never* see those Egyptians again. You will never again be bound by their chains. They will never again hold you in bondage. The Israelites could not have foreseen their march across the Red Sea when they were in Egypt building bricks without straw under the ruthless Egyptian taskmasters, but God did.

My friend, this message is for you and I too. When God takes us on a life-journey out of bondage, He tells us to stand firm, and He guarantees our deliverance. Complete, full, final deliverance.

God triumphs over fear.

The Israelites were free when they reached the other side of the Red Sea but fear kept them from living in freedom. They saw the miracles of God and yet they let fear control them. They watched the Lord send legions of frogs into Egypt, yet they feared He could not provide them food. They watched the Lord turn the Nile River to blood and then back to clean water again, yet they feared they would die of thirst. Fear caused the Israelites to turn their backs on God and fashion idols of bronze and gold.

What things are you afraid of?

_____

_____

_____

The very things we fear are the very things God uses to stretch our faith, but often times we don't give Him the opportunity because we pull back and take things into our own hands. We become afraid and then we think that our plan is better or safer than what God has in mind. That's where the idols come into play. The Israelites fashioned idols of bronze and gold because they didn't trust the Lord. They thought that they would get what they wanted by worshipping a golden calf instead of praying to the Almighty God.

We do the same thing. It might not be a golden calf, but we have our own idols. We are afraid we won't have enough money for the electric bill, so we use a credit card. We are afraid people will know our marriage is struggling, so we create a façade of the happily married couple, hosting parties and leading a small group.

What idols do you fashion when you are afraid?

_____

_____

_____

There is no idol that is a match for the Creator of the Universe. He is not surprised by the circumstances in our lives, so rest assured that He has a plan.

What does 2 Timothy 1:7 (NKJV) say about fear?

_____

_____

_____

I think that fear is the number one tool that Satan uses to shut us down. What better way to thwart God's plan than to instill doubt and fear in regards to the process or the outcome? But faith is so much bigger than fear. Not sure? Just ask Abraham on his way back down the mountain with his son after God provided the sacrifice. Or ask David after defeating Goliath. Or ask Peter after his experience walking on water. Do you want freedom? Then don't be afraid, my friend. Stand firm.

Remember the story at the beginning of the chapter about my bike, the great green bike with the flowered banana seat? I used to ride my bike in search of freedom. I don't have that bike anymore, but I do still have a really cool bike. It's pink camouflage. I don't ride in search of freedom anymore, though. I ride to enjoy the freedom I live in every day.

chapter 2. hope for freedom.

I remember the day vividly. It was my son's sixteenth birthday. We had the first appointment at the Department of Motor Vehicles for him to take his driver's test. He was so nervous. I was nervous, too, because I knew I was going to have a wreck on my hands (no pun intended) if he didn't pass. After the test we drove home, he dropped me off and then drove off by himself to school. He passed. I stood on the porch for a long time after he pulled out looking into the direction he drove off thinking about how much I love that boy and how proud I am of him.

I was struggling with some depression in my life at that time. The year prior I had experienced a series of tragic events that were difficult within themselves, but they also brought me face to face with my dark past and sent me into a downward spiral. I had held it together pretty well, or so I thought, but on this special day, of all days, it all came crashing down. I went back in the house and started to plan my escape. I spent all day wrestling with the plan. With each passing hour my anxiety grew higher and higher. I wanted to die desperately and escape the pain I couldn't seem to overcome. I had lost all hope of ever living again. Never in a million years would I have thought I would be at that place where I would be willing to taking my own life. I had always been a survivor. It was truly the darkest hour in my life.

Describe a dark time in your life. Maybe you found yourself without a job for several months. Maybe your spouse left you alone after years of what you thought was a happy marriage. Maybe you've experienced a serious illness. Maybe you know the pain of the depression I described above.

_____

_____

_____

In my darkest hour I needed God desperately. I knew He was there; I just didn't know how to find Him. The good news is that I didn't need to find Him. He was there all along, waiting to breathe new life back into me.

God takes us by the hand.

Read Ezekiel 37. It is a very rich text, so you may want to read it through more than once. Remember to mark words or verses that stand out to you. This will help when you go back to journal and answer questions.

Let me give you some back story on what was happening at the time the Lord gave this vision to the prophet Ezekiel. All of Israel was in captivity. There was a remnant in Judah, but the vast majority of the Jews had been exiled to Babylon. Ezekiel was in Babylon preaching of God's judgment on Israel for their repeated sin as a people. He was also preaching to surrounding nations of the judgment God would bring on them for their wickedness. In Ezekiel 36 the prophecy takes a turn to a message of hope and restoration.

What did the Lord speak to you as you read Ezekiel 37?

_____

_____

_____

_____

_____

Look at Ezekiel 37:1-2. Where specifically did the Lord take Ezekiel?

_____

_____

When we are in the darkest of valleys, we pray to the Lord and ask Him to get us out of the valley. Often times, instead, He takes us by the hand and leads us to the center of the valley. He leads us to the center where there is nowhere to hide, nowhere to turn away from the desolation, no way to deny the reality. And then He leads us back and forth. He intends for us to spend some time in the valley, and not just in one place. He wants us to walk back and forth, to see it all. In fact, He leads us to take steps forward and steps backward. When we are in need of healing from a dark place in our lives, our tendency is to avoid those places, often burying hurts with the intention that they be buried forever. Though that may seem the less painful route, each hurt in our lives was put there for a specific purpose, and God doesn't want us to miss a part of His divine plan.

There are a couple of words and phrases that I think were chosen carefully in these verses. In Ezekiel 37:1 the NIV translation uses the word "set." *"The hand of the Lord was upon me, and He brought me out by the Spirit of the Lord and set me in the middle of a valley; it was full of bones."* This word, set, implies something done deliberately and with purpose. God doesn't just take us anywhere in the valley. He "sets" us someplace specifically. Ezekiel 37:2 in the NIV translation uses the phrase "He led me back and forth." Sometimes God intends for us to spend time in the valley, and not just in one place. It is often in the valley where we find ourselves learning to look up and trust His leading.

What specifically did Ezekiel see as described in verse 2?

_____

_____

Ezekiel saw everything in the valley. Nothing was hidden from him. And he saw that the bones in the valley were very dry. They had been there awhile, sitting and rotting. There was no mistake that they were dead. When we ignore and bury our hurts, that is exactly what happens to them. They sit and rot and a piece of our soul dies with each hurt we bury.

God breathes new life.

Read Ezekiel 37:3. What was the question?

_____

_____

What was the answer?

_____

_____

The Lord asked Ezekiel if it was possible for the bones to live. Can you imagine what would have gone through your mind had you been in Ezekiel's position? I think my response would weigh in on the practical side and I would say, "Of course not. The bones are dry and dead."

But not Ezekiel. He shows us the true essence of faith. "Lord, you alone know." He was in the middle of a valley of bones, yet his faith was not shaken. He knew that even under those unlikely conditions, God was still the Master, still on the throne, still in control. Doesn't that give you confidence? God knows all things, so we don't have to know. We just have to have faith.

What shakes your faith?

_____

_____

_____

_____

_____

What can you do to restore your faith when it is shaken?

_____

_____

_____

Ezekiel did not allow his faith to be shaken. Instead he relied on what he knew to be true about the Lord. He trusted in His sovereignty. He trusted in His plan.

Read Ezekiel 37:5. What promise did the Lord make?

_____

_____

"This is what the Sovereign Lord says to these bones: 'I will make breath enter you and you will come to life.'" The Lord said, "I will." That is a promise from the Lord because the Lord always does what He says He is going to do. Anyplace you see the words 'I will' coming from the Lord in the Bible, you are reading a promise. The promise was amazing: I promise to come to you and breathe new life into your old, dried up bones. In the midst of our darkness, He promises to come and breathe new life into us. New life. He doesn't just regenerate the old life. He doesn't put on a bandage or do plastic surgery. He breathes brand new life into our tired, lonely, dried up places. And that, my friend, is sweet freedom.

God makes us one.

Read Ezekiel 37:15-16. What did the two sticks represent?

_____

_____

One stick represented the nation of Judah, the southern kingdom, and the other stick represented the nation of Israel, the northern kingdom.

What does Ezekiel 37:19 say will happen to the two sticks?

_____

_____

The two sticks becoming one symbolizes the joining of the southern kingdom and the northern kingdom into one nation of Israel. They were one people, God's chosen people, and He did not want them to be divided. God wants to do the same thing in our lives. In our quest to bury our hurts and failures and move on with our lives, we subconsciously compartmentalize our lives and end up with two distinct selves warring against each other - the self that has buried the hurt and failure and moved on, and the self that is still silently hurting. God does not desire for us to live our lives with these distinct selves apart from one another. He created us to be complete individuals, and that includes our hurts and failures.

What things in your life have you buried or hidden because you did not want them to be a part of the life you are living?

_____

_____

_____

_____

_____

What would it take to "fuse the sticks" together?

_____

_____

_____

_____

_____

_____

In my own journey, God used a series of tragedies to bring me to the center of the valley, and He intended for me to spend some time there. He wanted me to see all of the parts and pieces of my life, good and bad. My past and my hurts are an important part of who I am and God's plan for my life. He wanted to unite them all and make me whole. He wanted me to experience a new life He had waiting for me. And do you know what I found in this wonderful new life He had waiting for me? Freedom that I didn't even know existed!

part two. forgiven.

forgiven. one who has been pardoned. one who no longer feels resentment against.

"If you, O Lord, kept a record of sins, O Lord, who could stand? But with you there is forgiveness; therefore you are feared."

Psalm 130:3-4

God does not keep a record of wrongs. To hold back forgiveness serves only to keep us from fully experiencing the freedom God intended.

Finally, at age fifteen, after the Washington DC trip, I had all I could take, and I attempted to take my life. I did not die that day, but it did precipitate the end of my abuse. I never returned to the apartment.

In the absence of the abuse, I was left with the open wounds of all that had happened to me. In order to deal with the pain I fell into anorexia, bulimia, self-harm, and another suicide attempt. Still, I forged on.

I finished high school and went away to college. When I went away to college, I shut the door on the past and vowed I would never look back. Or so I thought. I finished college, started a career, met my husband, and was introduced to Jesus. He took me to church and introduced me to his friends. In them I saw a peace and a joy I had not ever experienced. I wanted what they had. So on November 4th, 1990 I gave my heart to Jesus and accepted Him as my Lord and Savior. I was married the next year.

Things just seemed to fall into place in my new life. My husband and I moved to Nashville, had our first child, adopted our second child, and third, and fourth. I was living the life that I had dreamed of. I was happily married, had four beautiful, healthy children, a ministry I loved. I was Sunday School teacher, PTO president, marathon runner, and IronMan triathlete. I could juggle all the balls and do it well. Everyone wanted the life that I had. What they didn't know was that I was living with a secret that was crushing me. I had created this façade of a life, the life I wanted, but it wasn't the life God intended me to live.

chapter 3. freedom opens our eyes.

Lord, thank you for being my Rock. You are forever faithful, loving me even when my faith is wavering. Thank you for being trustworthy, never changing, always loving me. Help me to rest with these truths today — the truths of your love, trustworthiness, and steadfastness.

God, I am so conflicted. I want to let go of all the pain and all of the lies, but I don't know how. I have lived with them for so long that they seem like an indelible part of me. If I am able to let go of the lies, what goes in their place?

--An entry from my personal journal

Have you ever struggled with the truth? I have. I've struggled with believing I am who God says I am – royalty, chosen, beloved, forgiven. I've struggled with believing God will never leave me or forsake me, regardless of what I have done or failed to do. I've struggled with believing that God has a plan and a purpose for my life.

What truths do you struggle with?

_____

_____

_____

God does not leave us alone.

Read 2 Kings 6:8-18. What did the Lord speak to you as you read this passage?

_____

_____

_____

_____

This is the scenario: the King of Aram is enraged because Elisha keeps tipping off the King of Israel as to his battle plans, allowing the Israeli army to circumvent attack. In order to solve the problem, instead of going after the King of Israel, the King of Aram decides to go after Elisha. Once Elisha is out of the picture, the Israeli army will be at his mercy. When he finds Elisha, the King of Aram sends the Aramean army to surround the city where he was found. At dawn, Elisha's servant goes outside and sees that they are surrounded.

Have you ever felt surrounded, trapped, in a situation with no plausible way out? Describe one or more of those times. What was the scenario leading up to it? How were you trapped? Who was with you? How did you feel?

_____

_____

_____

_____

_____

The Bible is filled with promises that the Lord is always with us and will never leave us.

Deuteronomy 31:6 - "Be strong and courageous. Do not be afraid or terrified because of them, for the Lord your God goes with you; He will never leave you nor forsake you."

Joshua 1:5 - "No one will be able to stand against you all the days of your life. As I was with Moses, so I will be with you; I will never leave you nor forsake you."

Isaiah 41:10 - "So do not fear, for I am with you; do not be dismayed, for I am your God. I will strengthen you and help you; I will uphold you with my righteous right hand."

Jeremiah 1:19 - "'They will fight against you but will not overcome you, for I am with you and will rescue you.' declares the Lord."

Matthew 28:20 - " …And surely I am with you always, to the very end of the age."

Many times we feel as if we are on our own. It is in those times that we must rely on what we know to be true instead of what we feel.

In 2 Kings 6:16-17, Elisha tells his servant two important things. First, he tells him not to be afraid. Second, he tells him that "those who are with us are greater than those who are with them." Those two statements tell us some things about Elisha's character. He is courageous. But why is he courageous? Because his faith is firmly rooted in a God who is bigger than any circumstance!

How big is your God? Is your God big enough for your circumstances?

_____

_____

_____

We can become so consumed with our circumstances that they become greater in our mind than even our God. But never forget, my friend, that your God is the Creator of the universe, the One who breathed life into you, the Christ who hung on a cross for you, and NOTHING is too big for Him.

Use the space below to journal a prayer about what you have learned from this passage. You can use one of the prompts below to get started:

- Lord, forgive me for not trusting you with …
- Lord, I know you are big enough to handle …
- Lord, you are God, and I am not. Help me …

_____

_____

_____

_____

_____

God gives us eyes to see.

Read 2 Kings 6:17. Write the verse below.

_____

_____

_____

Elisha prayed. He prayed that his servant would have eyes to see. Elisha didn't know what his servant would actually see, but he was praying for him to have faith that God was big enough. I like to imagine the smile on Elisha's face when the Lord made visible the legions of armies surrounding him. You see, this vision wasn't only for the servant, but it was also a confirmation of Elisha's faith. It's as if God were saying, 'Yes, Elisha, I've got this. Your faith has saved you from this enemy army.'

Elisha had the faith to see what the world could not. In what area of your life do you need that kind of faith? Where do you need to see what the world cannot?

_____

_____

_____

How have you seen your faith rewarded? What visible signs have there been of God's response to your faith? Try to think specifically of a time when you really put your faith to the test and God showed up to confirm your faith.

_____

_____

_____

There is something else to see in those legions of armies in verse 17. God could have shown Elisha and his servant anything – a physical barrier like a wall, the enemy army thrown into confusion, but God showed Elisha a legion of armies at their ready because He wanted Elisha to know he was not alone.

When are you most vulnerable to feel alone?

_____

_____

_____

Who makes up your army to surround you when you feel alone?

_____

_____

_____

God created us to be in community with one another. Refer back to the verses in the previous section. God is always with us, and He places people in our lives to walk alongside as while we are here on earth.

God hears us when we call.

When you are up against the enemy army, what is your first response?

_____

_____

_____

I admit that sometimes my first response when I sense danger or difficulty is to jump in and try to solve the problem on my own. I have expended so much energy trying to do things in my own strength. But Elisha prayed, and God answered him with a legion of armies.

Read 2 Kings 6:18. Seeing that the enemy was coming to attack, Elisha prayed again. This time he prayed for the enemy army to be struck blind, and again, the Lord answered his prayer.

What do you think it is about Elisha's prayers that God answered so readily?

_____

_____

_____

Elisha had unwavering faith. He expected God to show up big.

James 1:5-6 says, "If any of you lacks wisdom, he should ask God, who gives generously to all without finding fault, and it will be given to him. But when he asks, he must believe and not doubt, because he who doubts is like a wave of the sea, blown and tossed by the wind."

Read Mark 9:19-24. What was Jesus' rebuke?

_____

_____

_____

Jesus rebuked the people for their unbelief. He called them an "unbelieving generation" and was insulted when the father of the boy said, "*If* you can?" He reminds the crowd that all things are possible for those that believe, and in doing so he asserts His position as Lord.

How does the father in the passage respond to His rebuke?

_____

_____

_____

God requires only that we have faith and believe. There is no "If you can" when it comes to our Lord. Jesus said in verse 23, "Everything is possible for Him who believes." That's all it takes. We don't have to DO anything because the power to do all things comes from the Lord.

If you struggle with trying to do it all on your own, pray this prayer with me and make a commitment to make prayer your first response:

Lord, I admit that I like to handle things on my own. I know that you are always with me because your Word promises it. I also know you put others in my life to walk alongside me when I feel alone. Today, I confess my tendency to go it alone, and I commit to reaching out to you and others you have placed in my life when I am faced with difficulty.

At the beginning of the chapter I included an excerpt from one of my personal journals. I was questioning God about the truth. The following excerpt was God's response to me on that same day:

Pain becomes relief. Fear becomes courage. Self-hate becomes self-love. Shame becomes acceptance. Powerlessness becomes empowered. Lies become the TRUTH.

So this is my truth. I lived a childhood of abuse and neglect. They play a part in who I am today, but they have no power over me. They do not define me. The effects of these things are pain, fear, self-hate, shame, powerlessness, and lies. I do not have to live with these effects. I can let them go and replace them — God can replace them — with relief, courage, self-love, acceptance, empowerment and truth. So the question is, "How do I let go?" Forgiveness. It's time to forgive and let go. It's time to take the power back. It's time to put the pain, fear, self-hate, shame, and lies back on the one to whom they belong. It's time to receive relief, courage, self-love, acceptance, empowerment, and TRUTH. It's time to believe the TRUTH.

--An entry from my personal journal

What is your truth?

_____

_____

_____

_____

_____

_____

chapter 4. freedom in forgiveness.

Forgiveness is complex, or perhaps we just make it that way. Sometimes we forgive easily because the offense is minor or involves someone we love. Or it comes easily because we are convicted of what Christ did for our forgiveness on the cross, and we feel we must forgive, as if it is our duty. Other times forgiveness is difficult. We are so deeply wounded that we cannot muster what it takes to say those three simple words, "I forgive you."

When do you find it difficult to forgive?

_____

_____

_____

I admit that I have struggled with forgiveness. I was deeply wounded by my father. The abuse I suffered at his hands is unforgivable. Isn't it? It was unfair. Demoralizing. Evil. But unforgiveable? Even deeper was the wound from my mother. I felt so rejected. Abandoned. Where was her protection? Where was her compassion? Where was her love? I desperately wanted her to be there for me. Her absence left me like helpless prey waiting to be devoured. It is unforgivable. Isn't it?

Even as I write these words I am struck with the image of Jesus, my Lord, hanging on the cross, blood pouring from His body, looking down at me as I stand at His feet and saying, "Is this enough?" Is. This. Enough. Is this enough blood to cover your father's sins? Is this enough blood to cover his abuse, his lies, his apathy? What about your mother, Michele? Is this enough blood to cover her sins? Is it enough to cover her abuse, her neglect, her apathy?

Wow. Talk about conviction. If the blood of my Lord was poured out to cover ALL sins for ALL people, who am I to withhold my forgiveness?

What offenses are you still holding on to and who do you need to forgive?

_____

_____

_____

God's love is not conditional.

Read John 8:1-11. Pay special attention to the spoken words and also to the setting and the actions of the people in this passage. Try to get the feel of how this encounter took place.

Have you ever felt condemned? What was it like? Who did you feel was condemning you?

_____

_____

_____

Now let's look at the other side. Have you ever condemned anyone? Who were you condemning? What were the circumstances? What was the offense?

_____

_____

_____

Jesus was teaching in the temple court, and the Pharisees brought a woman who had been caught in adultery. They asked Jesus what they should do with her, knowing that the law said to stone her. Jesus very calmly bent down and began to write in the dirt with His finger. We have no idea what He might have been writing, but my guess is nothing in particular. I think He was taking time to contemplate the moment and to give time for the crowd to die down as they awaited His response. Then He stood up and told the crowd that the one without sin could throw the first stone. He knelt back down to draw in the dirt again and waited. Some Bible scholars suggest that Jesus may have been writing the sins of the men that brought the woman to Him. One by one, beginning with the oldest members of the crowd, they all turned and walked away. When they were all gone He stood up and asked the woman where everyone went. He asked her if anyone had condemned her. She responded that no one had, and Jesus did something amazing. He gave her assurance that He did not condemn her either, and He sent her on her way and told her to leave her life of sin. Her freedom rested in His offer of forgiveness.

Jesus was not surprised by this woman's sin, nor is He surprised by ours. He sees the sin in our lives, and He sees the forgiveness we are withholding. The same grace and forgiveness that He extended to the woman, He extends to all of us.

1 Timothy 2:5-6 says, "For there is one God and one mediator between God and mankind, the man Christ Jesus, who gave Himself as a ransom for *all people.*"

In Romans 5:18-19 we read, "Consequently, just as one trespass resulted in condemnation for all people, so also one righteous act resulted in justification and life for all people. For just as through the disobedience of the one man the many were made sinners, so also through the obedience of the one man *the many* will be made righteous."

Neither of these verses places a condition on the sin or the sinner. Neither should we. But don't take my word for it. Take the word of the Maker of heaven and earth.

"He has shown you, O mortal, what is good. And what does the Lord require of you? To act justly and to love mercy and to walk humbly with your God." Micah 6:8

part three. FREE.

FREE. enjoying personal rights or liberty, as a person who is not in slavery. clear of obstructions or obstacles.

"It is for freedom that Christ has set us free. Stand firm, then, and do not let yourselves be burdened again by a yoke of slavery."

Galatians 5:1

God created each of us uniquely individual with a plan and a purpose. He desires nothing more than to see us live out the life He intended us to live.

I don't like to say that all good things must come to an end, but in my case it was the truth. In 2012 I faced a series of tragic events that brought me a new reality. I lost two dear friends — one to suicide and one to murder. And my fifteen year old daughter was diagnosed with stage III-B ovarian cancer.

Unless you have actually experienced it yourself, you have no idea what it is like to stand in a hospital hallway and hear a doctor say, "Your daughter has cancer." Nothing prepares you to hear those words. And yet they were the words and the reality I had to face. And so relying on my faith and friends, I drew the strength and courage I needed to care for my sick daughter. For six months she and I lived at Vanderbilt Children's Hospital where she underwent intensive inpatient chemotherapy five days a week. At the end of six months, in the fall of 2012, there were no signs of cancer remaining in her body.

It was a time of celebration, but I was without resource. Depression had begun to set in, and my perfectly maintained exterior was starting to crack. The new trauma in my life resurrected the old trauma in my life. The resources I had been using to keep my secrets had dissolved. I was in such emotional pain that I physically hurt. When I was finally able to speak I called my husband and said, "I can't do this anymore. You have to help me." That was all I could manage to say. I was the one who did it all, and I had never asked for help before.

When I was at my lowest, I couldn't even find God. I was numb. I still opened my Bible every day, but the words wouldn't penetrate my mind or heart. I still wrote prayers in my journal. There are pages upon pages asking, "Where are you, God?" and pleading with Him to let me hear his voice. I knew He was there, I just didn't know how to find Him.

I reached out for help and spent the next six months uncovering all of the secrets I had buried for years. The shame and self-loathing I felt were unbearable. I just wanted my old life back. I did not want to accept that the part of me that had endured such a painful pas was indeed part of my story and a part of what makes me whole.

It took time for me to realize that the shame I felt was not mine to bear, but belonged to the ones who hurt me. Isaiah 61:7 reminds me, "Instead of your shame you will receive a double portion, and instead of disgrace you will rejoice in your inheritance. And so you will inherit a double portion in your land, and everlasting joy will be yours."

It took time for me to finally begin to accept that I was not disgusting, used, and tainted. I learned to believe Psalm 139:14, "I praise you because I am fearfully and wonderfully made; Your works are wonderful, I know that full well."

It took time for me to learn how to integrate the part of my life I had kept secret for so long with the life I was actually living. In a sense I had to rebuild my identity. I was living the life that I wanted to live – or at least the one I thought I wanted. I was in a cycle of perpetual motion, always doing, always striving. And if it wasn't perfect, it was a failure, which meant I was a failure. Everything had to be perfect.

I had to finally come out of the denial that the perfect life that I had created was not the life God intended for me. When I escaped the life of my childhood and teens, I shut the door on it. I moved away and it didn't exist anymore. God let me live in that denial for a while, then He got a hold of me and said, "No more. I created you. All of you. You have a story that I have given you for the purpose of revealing My Glory."

chapter 5. the price of FREEDOM.

On February 18, 2012 I loaded my suitcase into the car and said good-bye to my family, not knowing when I would see them again. The days ahead were filled with uncertainty. I was trusting in one thing, and that was that God *was* certain of the days ahead.

Describe a time in your life when you were uncertain about the days ahead? Maybe you find yourself in that place now. Where was (or is) your faith during this time?

_____

_____

_____

God chooses each of us.

Read Luke 1:26-38. This may be another familiar passage. Read it slowly and imagine that you have never heard the story before.

What is your response to this passage as you let it fall on fresh eyes?

_____

_____

_____

It occurs to me that Mary was taken completely off guard by the angel Gabriel. She was not going about her day expecting to be interrupted by a heavenly visitation. In fact, the Bible says she was "greatly troubled" at the angel's words. I don't know what you think, but "greatly troubled" seems like a very reasonable response to me. Then something interesting happens. Mary engages in conversation with the angel. She asks him a question, and in doing so acknowledges that what he is saying is something bigger than her. Finally something incredible happens. With little more than what the angel had said to her, Mary gave herself fully over to the will of the Lord.

Write Luke 1:38.

_____

_____

_____

What incredible faith and submission! You know Mary must have had a million other questions, yet she tossed them to the wind and gave herself over to the Lord's divine plan.

In the above scenario you described of an uncertain time in your life, what questions did you have?

_____

_____

_____

We don't usually think of Mary as someone in bondage, but stick with me on this one for a minute or two. Mary was in bondage as much as we are all in bondage without Christ.

The Bible says in John 8:36, "So if the Son sets you free you will be free indeed."

2 Corinthians 3:17 says, "Now the Lord is the Spirit, and where the spirit of the Lord is, there is freedom."

In Galatians 5:1 we read, "It is for freedom that Christ has set us free. Stand firm, then, and do not let yourselves be burdened again by a yoke of slavery."

So, Christ came why?

_____

_____

_____

Christ came to set us free!! You won't be able to convince me that Mary didn't feel the pressure of her situation and a sense of bondage. It was a scandal. She was single. Betrothed. And pregnant! Do you not think people stared as she walked down the street and whispered as she walked past? Do you think even her parents found it hard to believe? We don't read about them in the Bible, but as a parent of teenage girls that I trust, I think even then I would find the story suspicious. What do you think Joseph's reaction was when he first heard? We know he eventually got his own angelic visitation, but what about before then? Was he angry with Mary? Did he believe her? Was he hurt? I wonder if she was even free to walk about town or if she became a recluse in her home.

Have you ever found yourself in a situation like Mary's, on the verge of something wonderful and yet, something is stealing your joy? What were the circumstances that prevented you from celebrating?

_____

_____

_____

Mary had just received the most amazing news of her life, yet because of the nature of her situation she could not share it publicly. I would imagine that she wanted to shout it from a mountaintop but instead had to keep it private.

I don't think Mary's scrutiny ended when Jesus was born. She was left to convince the world that her screaming infant was the Son of God. Yet somehow I think she was able to hold her head high knowing that is exactly who He was.

Describe a time in your own life when, despite the scrutiny of others, you had complete confidence that you were doing exactly what God wanted you to do?

_____

_____

_____

God's will is worth it.

Read Luke 2:1-20. Was it worth it? All of the scrutiny and staring and whispering? All of the unknown? Look again at verse 19, "But Mary treasured up all these things and pondered them in her heart." It was worth it.

In the last segment you wrote about a time when you followed God's will despite the scrutiny of others. Was it worth it? Why?

_____

_____

_____

Sometimes God has monumental tasks for us, but most of the time what He requires is very simple. Read Deuteronomy 10:12-13.

List the things from this passage that the Lord asks of you?

_____

_____

_____

_____

What the Lord requires is very simple – to fear Him, to walk in His ways, to love Him, to serve Him, and to obey His commands. Five simple things are all He requires. We make it so much more complicated!

Rewrite Deuteronomy 10:12-13 inserting your name where it says 'Israel'.

_____

_____

_____

_____

_____

By personalizing this verse we are able to hear it as a directive from the Lord. Commit this verse to memory and recall it at times when you feel overwhelmed. Remember that it doesn't have to be so complicated!

It was six months before I returned to my family. In that time I missed birthdays and holidays, milestones, performances, sporting events, and day to day life. Yes, my search for freedom came with a high price. I can never get those moments back. But if I had never taken the risk, I would have never found the freedom God intended me to live in at the end of the journey.

chapter 6. FREEDOM is a choice.

It was a warm, September day. We were sitting in the shade on a wooden bench under a gazebo. We sat facing each other, but I could not look up at my husband. I was about to tell him the secret from my past that I had kept for more than thirty years. This secret carried with it so much shame, and I was scared. No, I was terrified. What if he was angry? What if he was disgusted? What if he decided it was all too much? Ultimately, that was my biggest fear – that he would leave me. Yet I made the decision to step out in faith beyond my fears and tell him.

What is your biggest fear? How does it keep you from walking in freedom?

_____

_____

_____

God loves each of us.

Read John 11:1-44. The story of Lazarus. I've heard it more than a dozen times, yet as I heard it in church that day and then read it again, the Spirit pricked my heart, and I saw it afresh, with new eyes.

When was the last time you read scripture with fresh eyes? If it has been awhile since you have felt the Spirit prick your heart with a new perspective, say a prayer asking the Lord to help you read His Word with fresh eyes and an open heart. Record the verses that speak to you from this passage and the new perspective the Spirit gave you.

_____

_____

_____

There are several verses that hold valuable truth that I want us to look at together for the remainder of the chapter.

Verse 3, "Lord, the one you love is sick." Aren't we also the ones He loves?

Jeremiah 31:3 confirms that we are the ones He loves, "The Lord appeared to us in the past, saying: 'I have loved you with an everlasting love; I have drawn you with unfailing kindness.'"

In Matthew 10:30-31 we read of our worth to the Lord, "And even the very hairs of your head are all numbered. So don't be afraid; you are worth more than many sparrows."

Verse 4, "When he heard this, Jesus said, "This sickness will not end in death. No, it is for God's glory so that God's Son may be glorified through it." He delivers us! He does mighty things in our lives to bring glory to Himself and freedom to us. This truth still lives on today!

Verse 6, "So, when He heard that Lazarus was sick, He stayed where He was two more days." Jesus works in His timing. We want Him to come to our aid right now, yet it is in His timing that our deliverance is made perfect.

With what things are you trying to rush His timing?

_____

_____

_____

Verse 15, "And for your sake I am glad I was not there, so that you may believe. But let us go to him." Sometimes we need to be reminded how great His power is. He knows we get caught up in our own circumstances, get overwhelmed, and need reminding that He has got it - He always has, and He always will.

God desires our trust.

Verse 22, "But I know that even now God will give you whatever you ask." These words were spoken by Martha to Jesus. Martha trusted Jesus completely. She trusted Him with her brother even in His death.

What do you need to trust Jesus with?

_____

_____

_____

Do you have the faith to believe He will take care of whatever you entrust to Him? If so, how can you be sure? If not, what is standing in your way?

_____

_____

_____

There is something else about Martha. She voiced something that is so relevant in our lives; it is the faith we say we have, but is it the faith we really have?

What is the faith you say you have?

_____

_____

_____

When is that faith challenged?

_____

_____

_____

It's so easy for us to declare our faith and trust in the Lord as long as it is just words, then when that faith is tested we let doubt creep in to challenge the truth we know.

Verses 34-35, "'Where have you laid him?" he asked. 'Come and see, Lord,' they replied. Jesus wept." Jesus is deeply compassionate. He cares about our pain. There is something very comforting in knowing that the God of the universe cares about my pain, that He weeps over my pain. God doesn't just tell us these things about Himself in stories where they apply only once. He uses the true stories to reveal His character. That is the Living Word! When we read the scripture it applies to our lives too! We have to take the time to let the Holy Spirit speak to us through the Word, and we have to be willing to hear what He says.

Verse 39, "'Take away the stone,' he said. 'But, Lord,' said Martha, the sister of the dead man, 'by this time there is a bad odor, for he has been there four days.'" But Lord?! Really?! What happened to the faith from verse 22? It was declared so confidently. Isn't that just like us, though? We declare our faith confidently with our words, but as soon as it gets tested our doubts rise to the surface.

What things cause you to doubt your faith?

_____

_____

_____

Verse 40, "Then Jesus said, 'Did I not tell you that if you believe, you will see the glory of God?'" Jesus reminds us of what He already said. How many times do we have to be reminded? We have the Word, we know what it says, and yet we say, "But Lord ..."

What are you saying "But Lord ..." to? "But Lord I can't ..." "But Lord if only ..." "I know you can, but Lord ..."

_____

_____

_____

As I began to deal with the trauma of my past I found myself saying, "But Lord." I consider myself a strong Christian, firmly rooted in the Word, and when it came down to putting that knowledge of the Truth to the test, I found myself doubting. I remember thinking, "I know you want me to live in freedom, *but Lord* I can't if that means letting go of my secret past. You aren't possibly big enough to help me overcome the pain, the shame, the humiliation." That's what it comes down to – do we believe that God is big enough?

Is God big enough to handle your "But Lord ..."?

_____

_____

_____

Verse 43, "When he had said this, Jesus called in a loud voice, 'Lazarus, come out!'" In this verse it's as if Jesus says, "Let me show you how big my God is." He calls for the dead man, and he came out of the tomb! The power of God is real and undeniable! The same God who created the universe is the same God who raised Lazarus from the dead and the same God that raised Christ from the dead. I believe He is big enough for whatever you and I have for Him.

In his letter to the Ephesians, Paul says, "I pray that the eyes of your heart may be enlightened in order that you may know the hope to which He has called you, the riches of His glorious inheritance in His holy people, and His incomparably great power for us who believe. That power is the same as the mighty strength He exerted when He raised Christ from the dead and seated Him at His right hand in the heavenly realms." (Ephesians 1:18-20) Did you read that? The same power that was used to raise Christ from the dead is alive in us today!

Does knowing that the same power that raised Christ from the dead is available to you change the things to which you might say, "But Lord …"? Explain.

God invites us to change clothes.

Verse 44, "The dead man came out, his hands and feet wrapped with strips of linen, and a cloth around his face. Jesus said to them, 'Take off the grave clothes and let him go.'" This verse is where Jesus shows us our part in freedom and in living. Jesus gave Lazarus his freedom and his life when He called him out of the grave. He came out, but he was bound up in all of the grave clothes. His hands and feet were wrapped with strips of linen. He even had a cloth covering his face; the Bible says it was wrapped around his face. Lazarus was alive, but he couldn't live in freedom as long as he was bound up in those grave clothes.

What grave clothes are you wearing? Is it a cloth of denial covering your face so that you refuse to see the truth? Do you have cloths of fear binding your feet, keeping you from stepping into the freedom God intended for you? Do you have cloths of idleness binding your hands – you don't know what to do so you do nothing? Or maybe your hands are wrapped in busyness, and you fill your time with so many things that you don't have time for the Lord or His freedom?

_____

_____

_____

I've worn grave clothes that looked like all of the above choices at some point. There was a point in my life where I was consumed with putting on a front of the woman who had it all together. The reality was that I was trying to cover up the shame and hurt of my secret past. I was living a façade of a life, and though filled with good things, it wasn't the life God intended for me to live. Until I was able to shed the façade and be real and honest, I could not walk in the freedom God had for me.

Whatever your grave clothes are, Jesus doesn't want you to wear them anymore. And the good news is that He doesn't expect us to remove them on our own. He sends people across our paths and creates Divine appointments for others to help us take off our grave clothes. Lazarus was surrounded by people that loved him when Jesus set him free. He didn't tell Lazarus to take his own grave clothes off and be on his way. He instructed the people that were close to him to take them off and let him go.

Can you imagine what Lazarus did when he was completely free? I can imagine there was a party in the streets! I can also imagine that there was a party in Heaven as the angels celebrated another life walking in freedom.

What does freedom look like for you?

_____

_____

_____

Freedom for me looked like letting down all my defenses, shattering all pretenses about the person I let everyone believe was the real me, and finally being honest with myself. I had created a great life, or so it appeared, but it wasn't the life God intended me to live. Why not, if it was so good? It wasn't good because it wasn't real. God creates us with a plan and a purpose. He wants us to live out that plan and purpose.

Do you have a sense of the plan and purpose God has for your life? Write about it here. If you are feeling lost about the plan and purpose God has for your life, journal a prayer asking God to reveal His plan and purpose for you.

_____

_____

_____

Maybe you are at a crossroads in your life, and you don't know who can help you with your grave clothes. You long to be free but need someone to come alongside you. Begin to pray now for the Lord's intervention that He would send that person into your life. Remember, God created us in community. He does not intend for us to do life alone.

As I told my story and divulged my secret back on that September day, my husband listened intently. When I was finished he took me into his arms and held me. I did it. I released the secret. I sobbed for what must have been an hour. Then he lifted my face to his and told me that he loved me. He told me that nothing would ever change his love for me. In that moment I experienced Jesus with skin on.

I am loved fully, as a woman with a painful secret past and years of living behind a façade. I am loved fully in spite of what has been done to me and in spite of what I have done. I am loved fully because I am uniquely crafted by the Creator of the universe with a story that He has written just for me. That, my friend, is the wonderful, pure, unconditional love of God our Father.

I am standing firm, seeking the Lord, listening for His direction, and living in freedom!

"I will stand at my watch
and station myself on the ramparts;
I will look to see what He will say to me ..."
Habakkuk 2:1

Acknowledgements

There are so many people to thank for the writing of this book. To my husband and children, Mark, Jade, Noah, Katie and Jonathon, thank you for believing in me and allowing me time to study and write. To Vicki, thank you for being my solid rock to lean on through this process. To Leigh, thank you for being my encourager and cheerleader. To the people that supported my campaign, you made possible what I could not have done on my own. Thank you Charles and Terri Hagood, Bill and Tina Davis, Rick and Lisa Lovins, Pat Dellario, Dominic Parente, Tammy Neisz, Lisa Ferrell, Joana Riddick, Sharon Jesse, Mark and Vicki Bowen, Tom Audy, Rachel Welch, Janet Chambers, Desneige VanCleve, Bobbie Coomer, Sheila Keltner, Barbara Elliot, Micki Johns Jennene Painter, Brenda Popplewell, Jill Popplewell, John and Jennifer Steen, Matt Hobdy, Cathy Graff, Kimberley Zimmerman, Kristi LaPointe, Wendy Lanphere, Heather Lake, Anna Hite, Donna Mule, Ashley Gorley, Paula Cowden, Melanie Smith, Brian Coomer, Beth Bozelli, Marian Griffin, Valerie Barr, Christen Lassiter. And to my anonymous donors, you know who you are, and I thank you for your support.

"I thank my God every time I remember you. In all my prayers for all of you, I always pray with joy because of your partnership in the gospel from the first day until now, being confident of this, that he who began a good work in you will carry it on to completion until the day of Christ Jesus."
Philippians 1:3-6

Printed in the United States
By Bookmasters